First published in this format 2014

Text: Alice Fisher
Jacket/Cover and Interior Design: Kimberly Adis
Interior Layout: Kimberly Shake
Cover Photographer: Alexandra Grablewski
Executive Editor, Series: Shawna Mullen
Assistant Editor, Series: Timothy Stobierski
Series Art Director: Rosalind Loeb Wanke
Series Production Editor: Lynne Phillips
Series Copy Editor: Barbara Cottingham

The Taunton Press
Inspiration for hands-on living®

The Taunton Press, Inc., 63 South Main Street,
PO Box 5506, Newtown, CT 06470-5506
e-mail: tp@taunton.com

Threads® is a trademark of The Taunton Press, Inc.,
registered in the U.S. Patent and Trademark Office.

The following names/manufacturers appearing in
DecoDen Bling are trademarks: Amazing Goop®,
Amazon℠, E6000®, Ebay℠, Etsy℠, Fimo®, Hello Kitty®,
Michaels®, Mod Podge®, Sculpey®

Library of Congress Cataloging-in-Publication Data in
progress

ISBN: 978-1-62710-887-4

Printed in the United States of America
10 9 8 7 6 5 4 3 2 1

contents

what is DecoDen?

What do smiling cupcakes, blushing bunnies, and cell phones have in common? If this sounds like the most unlikely combination of things, you might be surprised how fun and playful they are when they come together in the Japanese craft technique called DecoDen.

Born out of the Japanese kawaii (*cute*) obsession, DecoDen refers to the art of decorating objects in an over-the-top, whimsical style. Deco is short for decorate and den comes from the Japanese word *denwa*, meaning phone. Yes, this craze started with blinged-out cell-phone

cases, but the trend has spread to anything and everything, from compacts to hair barrettes to gaming devices to fingernails! Using either a homemade paste, silicone bathroom caulk, or special DecoDen crème called whip, crafters can adhere rhinestones, charms, or playful cabochons like mini-pastries, fruits, bows, or flowers to their objects of choice. The most closely related craft to compare it to would be mosaic, the art of embedding small tiles into grout to create a pattern or picture. The best part about DecoDen is that it appeals to crafters of all ages. If you can ice a cake, then you have the skills to DecoDen!

What You'll Need

You need just a few basic materials to get your DecoDen projects going. These crafts can be created easily with just your adhesive of choice and the embellishments, but to accomplish the more detailed designs, you'll need a few extra, simple tools to help with the finer features.

You can DecoDen pretty much anything that has a rigid surface. The most popular items include cell-phone cases, fingernails, handheld game devices, tablet or computer covers, and small compact mirrors. If the surface of that you choose to embellish is very slick, you might consider roughening it up a bit with sandpaper to allow the adhesive to have something to grab hold to.

adhesives

WHIP

Special adhesives meant for DecoDen projects that looks like cake frosting when applied. Whip comes in a variety of icing-like colors (usually white, pink, brown, and mint green) and is sold in what looks and feels like icing piping bags. Different tips create different whip designs and motifs, but the most common tip is the star tip that creates a traditional icing look.

WHITE SILICONE BATHROOM CAULK

When using silicone caulk, it's best to work in a well-ventilated room with open windows or even outside. Since you are working so intimately close to the caulk, wear a paper mask to avoid breathing in the harsh fumes and follow all of the label directions. You can either dispense the caulk into a piping bag, or you can cut off the tip and securely tape on a star-shaped piping tip.

NOTE: If working with silicone, it is advisable to wear a mask.

DIMENSIONAL FABRIC PAINT

This paint comes in squeeze bottles with a fine tip and is traditionally used to decorate t-shirts and other fabric goods. In DecoDen it is used to create a delicious, drippy chocolate effect. Caramel colors and whites are other fantastic choices. While the paint is wet, press a rhinestone, flat-back pearl, or cabochon into the paint and let it dry there for at least 24 hours (the paint is very thick, so drying takes time).

COLORED GLUE-GUN STICK

You will need a high-heat glue gun for this technique, but it is so worth it—the glue sticks allow you to get the same drippy effect as dimensional fabric paints, but in a much wider variety of colors. Just be careful to follow all package directions and do not to melt the surface to which you are gluing!

GLUE

Strong glue such as E6000® is perfect for attaching cabochons to your items when you don't want to use whip. It dries clear and creates a powerfully strong bond that will sustain a pretty significant impact. When working on small or narrow surfaces, use a toothpick to spread the glue around.

tools

PIPING BAG AND TIPS

These are perfect to use with your whip. You can either dispense whip into a piping bag or simply (but securely) tape a piping tip over the nozzle of a squeeze tube.

TWEEZERS OR WAX PENCIL

Either of these are perfect for picking up and placing tiny rhinestones on your projects.

SANDPAPER

Sandpaper is great for roughing up the surface of your project a bit before you begin gluing on your materials—removing the slickness that you often find on phone cases and other items will allow the adhesives and embellishments to attach more securely.

PLASTIC ORGANIZER

Perfect for organizing your cabochons, rhinestones, and other embellishments.

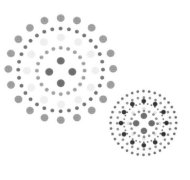

embellishments

CABOCHONS

A cabochon typically refers to a stone that has been polished as opposed to faceted. Cabochons historically have a convex form with a flat back. The flat back is the important aspect of cabochons used in DecoDen, as it allows them to attach unobtrusively to an object. Cabochons can be purchased from various websites (see Resources on p. 31) or made using silicone molds with resin, polymer clay, or melting colored sticks with a glue gun. See below for tips on making your own!

RHINESTONES

These add bling to any DecoDen project and come in both large and small varieties. Use them sparingly or in excess to add sparkle and whimsy to your project.

FLAT-BACK PLASTIC PEARLS

These work similarly to rhinestones, but add a softer, more romantic aesthetic.

MINI ERASERS

These popular Japanese export items are usually sold in the form of pastries, ice cream, cartoon characters, or really any kind of design. You can generally find them in a craft store, while cabochons are usually specialty items found exclusively online. Attach them to your projects like you would cabochons or rhinestones, but be careful: They tend to be bulkier than other embellishments.

FOUND ITEMS

Pretty much anything that strikes your fancy can be attached to a DecoDen project. If you are a flea-market maven, old buttons, keys, and small toys work well as embellishments. If you love mosaic, small ceramic pieces or mirrors are great. For the beach combers, seashells and sea glass look lovely on trinket boxes, flower pots, or even cell-phone cases. Experiment! Finding the perfect embellishments is half the fun of DecoDen!

Make Your Own Cabochons

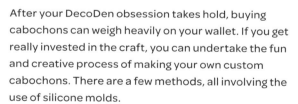

After your DecoDen obsession takes hold, buying cabochons can weigh heavily on your wallet. If you get really invested in the craft, you can undertake the fun and creative process of making your own custom cabochons. There are a few methods, all involving the use of silicone molds.

Silicone molds are often used in soap and chocolate making, and are available in small sizes. You can also buy molds that are specifically made for cabochons.

Polymer clays like Fimo® and Sculpey® can be pressed into silicone molds for quick cabochons. Because the clay is pre-colored, using it will save you the step of painting your cabochons once they are complete. To use polymer clay, all you need to do is fill the mold, pop the clay out of the mold once the shape is set, and bake in an oven according to package instructions. If you are using multiple colors of clay in a single cabochon, simply fill the mold with a small amount of clay at a time and use a toothpick or other small tool to move the colors into place.

You can also use resin to make cabochons that you want to paint by hand, which will really allow you to include a bit of yourself into everything that you make. The most commonly used product for DecoDen is called EasyCast Resin—because it is solvent free and low odor, it is ideal for indoor use. If you use resin to make cabochons, take note: Package instructions must be followed closely. Resin cabochons take around 72 hours to fully cure, so be sure to plan ahead.

Mod Melts are used with a high-heat glue gun to create your own cabochons. Squirt the melted liquid directly into a silicone mold, and in just 7 minutes the cabochon is dry. You can then remove the piece and paint as needed.

NOTE: To give your cabochons a nice shine, paint them with glossy Mod Podge® glue when finished.

Beach-Comber Phone Case

DESIGNED BY RACHAEL BECK

DecoDen isn't just about cute cupcakes and Japanese kawaii-inspired bling. Attach found objects like shells and sea glass to your phone to bring DecoDen to a truly elegant level.

SKILL LEVEL
Beginner

MATERIALS
Plastic phone case
Whip of your choice
Star-piping tip and piping bag
12–15 sea glass pieces
1 sea-inspired charm
Plastic pearls

TO MAKE BEACH-COMBER PHONE CASE

1. Pipe whip onto your phone case using the star-piping tip. *Since sea glass is translucent, try to create your piped design in neat, even rows as you will be able to see the pattern through your embellishments.*

2. Arrange sea glass pieces immediately, pressing them gently into the whip.

3. Leave space in the middle of the case to adhere a sea-inspired charm like a seahorse, starfish, or seashell. Embellish empty spaces with pearls just the way you like it! Let dry for 48 hours.

TIP If your sea glass varies in depth of color, you can arrange the pieces from darkest to lightest to create an ombré effect.

Cool Azul Mosaic Phone Case

DESIGNED BY KATHY CANO-MURILLO

Found objects can lend a beautiful vintage look to your DecoDen projects. Find objects that embody your personality, or whatever strikes you as pretty—just know that you're going to have a lot of curiosity directed your way whenever you whip out your phone!

SKILL LEVEL

Intermediate

MATERIALS

Plastic phone case

Whip of your choice

Plastic knife or palette knife

Plastic fork or piping tip

Tweezers or wax pencil

Small rhinestones, gems, and beads

10–12 found objects and cabochons (depending on size)

12 large rhinestones

Loose, fine glitter

TO MAKE COOL AZUL MOSAIC PHONE CASE

1. Apply a thick coat of whip to phone case. Spread it around the surface of the case with plastic knife or palette knife.
You might want to secure your phone case to your work surface with tape to keep it from moving while you are piping on the whip.

2. Use a fork or piping tip to create a texture in the whip. You can drag the tool in straight lines, zigzags, or waves to create texture.

3. Begin your design by using the tweezers or wax pencil to lay small rhinestones around the border of your phone case.

4. Place your large rhinestones and cabochons in the center area of your case.

5. Fill in empty spaces with rhinestones, gems, and beads.

6. Sprinkle glitter on top of the finished piece and set aside to let dry for 48 hours. Shake off excess glitter.

TIP Plan out your design before you begin. You can lay the cabochons and other embellishments on top of your object's surface and take a cell-phone pic to follow as you go. You can also trace the object onto paper and use that as your design guide.

B

A

TO MAKE UPCYCLED BLING TABLET CASE

1. Arrange key items on your case ahead of time to plan your design. Make sure to have enough embellishments on hand to create the design you have in mind before you begin gluing.

2. Apply glue to your phone case in 3" x 3" sections.

3. Following your pre-planned design, begin gluing the larger items into the glue, followed by the smaller filler elements. Use tweezers or a wax pencil to make it easier to place the small pieces.

4. In order to achieve this dense affect, keep filling in until you hardly see any spaces in between decorations.

5. Decorate your stylus by gluing on rows of small rhinestones. You can add one focal element to the top of the stylus, but keep the shaft simple so it's comfortable to hold.

6. For maximum strength, let glue dry for 24 hours.

Upcycled Bling Tablet Case

DESIGNED BY LINNETTE GARCIA

This tablet case **(A)** is a perfect example of DecoDen blinginess! With such a large surface area to cover, you can create decadence and excitement, adding personality to an otherwise plain object.

SKILL LEVEL

Intermediate

MATERIALS

Hard-shell tablet case and stylus

Glue

Rhinestones, various sizes

Broken jewelry pieces

Mismatched beads

Small toys

Charms

Tweezers or wax pencil

VARIATION

DESIGNED BY TAYLOR VASILIOU

The rhinestone variation **(B)** offers a balanced design. Glue your larger cabochons in place first, and let dry completely. Then glue the rhinestones in place, one at a time, in whatever fashion you like. You can arrange the rhinestones geometrically, you can alternate colors, or you can make it uniform— the design is completely up to you!

Plastic Fantastic Phone Case

DESIGNED BY CASSIE PERRY

Flowers, strawberries, and flowers . . . oh my! Indulge in Hello Kitty® to Winnie the Pooh and everything in between with this playful phone case **(A)**. Who would ever want to store her phone in her purse when it looks this cute?

SKILL LEVEL

Intermediate

MATERIALS

Hard-shell plastic phone case

Glue

25–30 small to medium plastic cabochons

Small rhinestones

Flat-back plastic pearls

Small beads

Tweezers or wax pencil

TO MAKE PLASTIC FANTASTIC PHONE CASE

1. Roughly plan out your design before you begin gluing pieces to the case.
Trace your phone case onto a piece of paper and lay larger cabochons and charms within the rectangle. This will help keep you organized as you glue.

2. Start gluing from the top of the case, working your way down. Glue all large pieces first, overlapping to create a layered look.

3. Once you have glued on all of your cabochons, fill in the open spaces with small rhinestones and flat-back plastic pearls. Use tweezers or wax pencil to make it easier to place them.

4. For maximum strength, let glue dry for 24 hours.

VARIATION

DESIGNED BY TAYLOR VASILIOU

The variation **(B)** uses fewer large cabochons, but fills the space with tiny rhinestones to a beautiful affect. Glue on your larger cabochons first and allow to dry; then, attach your rhinestones in whatever fashion you wish. As you can see, this phone case was created as a sister project to the rhinestone variation of the Upcycled Bling Tablet Case.

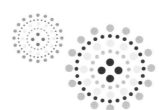

Chocolate Delight Phone Case

DESIGNED BY CASSIE PERRY

This phone case **(A)** looks good enough to eat! Luckily, it won't melt in your mouth, or in your hand.

SKILL LEVEL

Intermediate

MATERIALS

Mint green hard-shell phone case

Brown dimensional fabric paint

10–12 large chocolate, pastry, and ice cream cabochons

8–10 small rhinestones

8–10 flat-back plastic pearls

Tweezers or wax pencil

TO MAKE CHOCOLATE DELIGHT PHONE CASE

1. Cover about one quarter of the long edge of the cell phone case in brown dimensional fabric paint. Use the tip of the bottle to help spread the paint around.

Prep your surface. Make sure your surface is clean of any residue, oil, or particles. Some crafters like to sand their surfaces down to make them more receptive to whip or dimensional fabric paint, but it's not always necessary.

2. Holding the case from the other edge, create drip-like shapes with the paint, moving towards the opposite side of the case. Vary the length and thickness of the drips to give it a more natural look.

3. Immediately begin laying the large cabochons onto the wet painted surface. Focus on composition and create 2 or 3 groupings of items. *Give a bonbon or piece of chocolate cabochon a little dimensional paint drizzle to give it an extra chocolatey look.*

4. Drop small rhinestones and flat-back plastic pearls into the wet paint at various spots (use tweezers or a wax pencil if necessary). The rhinestones look especially nice at the bottom, rounded edge of the drips.

VARIATION

DESIGNED BY TAYLOR VASILIOU

To make the bunny variation **(B)** follow the same steps but instead of dripping the paint, layer it over the entire cell-phone case and swirl as through frosting a cake. Apply your beads and let dry—just be sure no one tries to sneak a bite!

Simply Sweet Phone Case

DESIGNED BY ASHLEY VALA

Sometimes less is more when it comes to DecoDen. This pastel beauty is a great example of how size and placement of like-colored cabochons creates a look that's simple and sweet.

SKILL LEVEL
Beginner

MATERIALS
Hard-shell phone case
Whip of your choice
Star-piping tip and piping bag
7 large plastic cabochons
10–12 small rhinestones
Tweezers or wax pencil

TO MAKE SIMPLY SWEET PHONE CASE

1. Apply whip to cell-phone case in large, rippled mounds using the star-piping tip.

2. Starting in the center begin arranging your cabochons by really nestling them into the whip at a 45 degree angle.

3. Place a few small rhinestones around the exposed whip, pressing down with tweezers or wax pencil. Let dry for 48 hours.

TIP In order to get that wavy icing look, don't pick up the piping tip from the case until the end of a row.

Kitty Video-Game Case

DESIGNED BY CATHIE FILIAN AND STEVE PIACENZA

Handheld game devices are almost as ubiquitous as the cell phone. Make your friends even more jealous when they see this decked-out case that makes playing video games more fun.

SKILL LEVEL

Beginner

MATERIALS

Wax paper

Whip of your choice

Star-piping tip and piping bag

White dimensional fabric paint

3 jumbo kitty gems

3 rhinestone bow cabochons

3 daisy flower cabochons

5 pink heart cabochons

Rhinestones

TO MAKE KITTY VIDEO-GAME CASE

1. Place a piece of wax paper between the top and bottom of the case to protect the bottom of the case.

2. Gather your embellishments and plan out the design of your case. *Artists Cathie Filian and Steve Piacenza made their own heart cabochons using Mod Melts, Mod molds, and acrylic paint. See p. 8 for instructions on how to make your own cabochons.*

3. Use a star-piping tip to apply the whip to the surface of the case.

4. Drizzle the white dimensional fabric paint all over the top of the case.

5. Embed the embellishments and rhinestones into the whip at a slight angle and set aside to dry for 48 hours. Remove the wax paper.

> **TIP** While the whip or dimensional paint is still wet and tacky, you can sprinkle fine glitter over it to add an extra layer of sparkle to your project.

Pretty-in-Pink Trinket Box

DESIGNED BY ERYNN TANIMOTO

Every girl needs a box to hold something—hair accessories, her favorite sweets, craft supplies, loose coins. Give an inexpensive box a playful makeover with some over-the-top pink girliness.

SKILL LEVEL

Beginner

MATERIALS

Plastic box

Whip of your choice

Star-piping tip and piping bag

7 large cabochons

Small rhinestones and flat-back plastic pearls

Tweezers or wax pencil

Pink dimensional fabric paint

TO MAKE PRETTY-IN-PINK TRINKET BOX

1. Remove lid from the box and apply whip to the top surface with a star-piping tip. (If the lid is hinged, just put wax paper between the top and bottom.)
If you are using silicone for whip and your plastic surface is slick, roughen up the surface of box lid a bit before applying.

2. Work from one corner to the opposite corner laying the cabochons into the whip at a slight angle.

3. Once your main pieces are in place, add small rhinestones and flat-back plastic pearls around the exposed whip. Use tweezers or a wax pencil to place the small pieces.

4. Let the whip harden for a about an hour before adding the dimensional fabric paint drips. Add drips in and around the crevices of the box top's iced edge. Let dry for 48 hours.

TIP If you are using a DecoDen whip product, it will harden into a shell first, but the inside will remain soft. You can begin the fabric paint drips after about an hour of drying time, but note that the whip will not fully dry all the way through until 48 hours later.

Perfectly Poppy Pencil Cup

DESIGNED BY ALICE FISHER

Desk accessories can seem sad and depressing, especially if you're staring at them while trying to do your math homework. Take a break from calculus and give a plain old pencil cup a little excitement.

SKILL LEVEL

Beginner

MATERIALS

Plastic cup

Turquoise dimensional fabric paint

25–30 rhinestones

Whip of your choice

Star-piping tip and piping bag

40–50 bugle beads

Tweezers or wax pencil

TO MAKE PERFECTLY POPPY PENCIL CUP

1. Starting about 1 inch down from top edge of cup, create drips of varying heights using dimensional fabric paint. Work all the way around the cup.
Use the tip of the squeeze tube to smooth and move paint around to your desired look.

2. Gently press rhinestones into the bottom of each paint drip. Let dry for 4 hours before applying the whip to avoid smudging.

3. Holding the cup horizontally in one hand, using the star-piping tip apply two bands of whip around the cup in between the top edge and the top of the drips. Create waves of whip in a continuous motion around the top edge.

4. Immediately drop bugle beads into the whip to give it a sprinkled look! Nestle them into the clay gently with the tip of tweezers, a wax pencil, or your fingernail. Let dry for 48 hours.

Glitzy-Girl Jewelry Box

DESIGNED BY CATHIE FILIAN AND STEVE PIACENZA

There's no better way to store your beloved bling than in a box worthy of holding it. Paint, then DecoDen a wooden jewelry box to match the precious contents it holds so safely.

SKILL LEVEL
Beginner

MATERIALS
Wooden jewelry box
Copper acrylic paint
Paint brush
Whip of your choice
Star-piping tip and piping bag
White glitter

2 jumbo rhinestone perfume bottles
1 large rhinestone bow
5 large rhinestone roses
7–10 plastic roses
2 large rhinestone hearts,
Various small pearls and gems

TO MAKE GLITZY-GIRL JEWELRY BOX

1. Paint a wooden jewelry box fully in copper acrylic paint. Let dry for about 30 to 45 minutes.

2. Once the painted box is dry, apply the whip to the top of the box using the star-piping tip.

3. Sprinkle white glitter over the whip to add another level of sparkle.

4. Embed the embellishments into the wet whip adhesive, beginning with the largest elements, and let dry for 48 hours.

> **TIP** Layering is key to a good DecoDen composition! Combining colors, shapes, and textures in an interesting way will make for a truly unique and decadent project.

Cherry-on-Top Clutch

DESIGNED BY CATHIE FILIAN AND STEVE PIACENZA

Mix unexpected patterns, colors, and motifs together in this eye-catching purse perfect for a night out on the town. Safari meets tutti-fruitti? Why not!

SKILL LEVEL

Intermediate

MATERIALS

Animal print hard-shell clutch

Pink dimensional fabric paint

Gold glitter

Pink whip

Star-piping tip and piping bag

4 large cherry cabochons

4 small cherry cabochons

8–10 heart gems, small flat-back plastic pearls and rhinestones

TO MAKE CHERRY-ON-TOP CLUTCH

1. Drizzle pink dimensional fabric paint in a drippy fashion loosely across two-thirds of the surface of the clutch.
You can cover the entire surface, but seeing the original color and pattern peaking through can add an unusual texture and dimension to your finished design.

2. Sprinkle a light layer of gold glitter over the wet paint. Let dry for 2 to 4 hours.

3. Apply pink whip with the star-piping tip on top of the dried drizzle and glitter.

4. Sprinkle gold glitter over the whip and embed the embellishments, pearls, and rhinestones into the whip. Let dry for 48 hours.

TIP If you make a mistake when applying whip or dimensional paint, wipe it away immediately with a damp paper towel or cloth.

Time, Sweet Time Clock!

DESIGNED BY CATHIE FILIAN AND STEVE PIACENZA

We decorate our homes with colors and patterns that we love, so why not decorate with our other obsessions . . . sugar, spice, and everything nice! Use store-bought and homemade cabochons to create a frame around a clock that literally looks good enough to eat.

SKILL LEVEL

Intermediate

MATERIALS

Round clock (any size)

Wax paper

Painter's tape

Brown dimensional fabric paint

Pink whip

Star-piping tip and piping bag

White glitter

25–30 small to medium sweets cabochons

Rhinestones

TO MAKE TIME, SWEET TIME!

1. To protect the face of the clock, cover the glass with wax paper and painter's tape.

2. Drizzle brown dimensional fabric paint loosely over the edge of the clock. Let dry about 2 to 4 hours.

3. Use the star-piping tip to apply dollops of pink whip all the way around the edge of the clock.

4. Sprinkle white glitter on top of the whip, then embed cabochons and rhinestones all the way around. *You want to place these cabochons flat onto the whip, not at an angle. Since this clock will hang on the wall, you want the cuteness to look you straight in the eye!*

5. After letting the design dry fully for 48 hours, remove tape and wax paper.

VARIATION

If you're not a dessert person, take a stab at this fun variation: Instead of sweets, place cabochons shaped like the foods that you like to eat at the times you find yourself eating them. What do you like to eat at breakfast, lunch, dinner, and all times in between? Can't find a cabochon shaped like your favorite snack? It's easy to make your own following the instructions on p. 8!

Rainbow Garden Photo Frame

DESIGNED BY CATHIE FILIAN AND STEVE PIACENZA

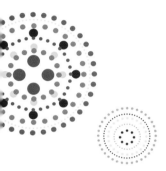

Create a beautiful, colorful bouquet of flowers on a heart-shaped picture frame. This frame would make a perfect Valentine's or Mother's Day gift!

SKILL LEVEL

Beginner

MATERIALS

40 various sized flower cabochons

Whip of your choice

Star-piping tip and piping bag

White dimensional fabric paint

White glitter

Flat-back plastic pearls

Hot-glue gun

White-rope trim

Scissors

TO MAKE RAINBOW GARDEN PHOTO FRAME

1. If you choose to make your own cabochons, follow the instructions on p. 8. Cabochons can be made with silicone molds and resin, polymer clay, or Mod Melts.

2. Cover the entire surface of the frame with white whip using the star-piping tip.

3. Add a light drizzle of white dimensional fabric paint over the freshly piped whip then sprinkle with white glitter.

4. Embed your store-bought or homemade flower cabochons into the whip in a rainbow pattern and fill empty areas with pearls.
You want to place these flowers flat onto the whip, not at an angle.

5. Hot-glue trim to the edge of the frame to give it a finished look. Let dry for 48 hours.

TIP Even though whip doesn't completely dry for 48 hours, the surface will harden to the touch rather quickly, so once you have applied the whip, embed your embellishments immediately.

TO MAKE HAPPY HALLWAY HOOKS

1. If you are using silicone and the surface of your hook is slick, you may want to roughen up the surface with sandpaper first. Pipe the whip in a swirl on the surface of the hook's face using the star-piping tip.

2. Press cabochons into the whip immediately and fill in around with small pearls.

3. Let dry completely for 48 hours before using.

Happy Hallway Hooks

DESIGNED BY ALICE FISHER

Decorate plain wall hooks with funny faces and pretty pearls. Let everyone in the family design their own hook so they always know exactly where to hang their coat, umbrella, or backpack.

SKILL LEVEL

Beginner

MATERIALS

Wall hooks with flat surface

Sandpaper (optional)

Pink whip of your choice

Star-piping tip and piping bag

Medium to large cabochons

Flat-back plastic pearls

Eye Love It Contact Lens Case

DESIGNED BY ALICE FISHER

Spend just a few minutes spicing up your contact lens cases with this super-simple embellishment. Next to your fancy cell phone case and compact mirror, don't let your contact lens case suffer from boredom.

SKILL LEVEL

Beginner

MATERIALS

Contact lens case

Whip of your choice

Star-piping tip and piping bag

Various embellishments (about 1" or less in diameter)

Mini flat-back plastic pearls and gems

TO MAKE EYE LOVE IT CONTACT LENS CASE

1. Pipe on a swirl or a dollop of whip onto each lid of your contact lens case using the star-piping tip. *When decorating contact lens cases, make sure to decorate the lids when they are screwed tightly onto the case. This way, you know that when your caps are on the case your cabochons and embellishments will all be facing the same direction.*

2. Press center cabochon or embellishment into the whip (either flat or at a slight angle), then add small gems or pearls around the edges. Let dry for 48 hours.

VARIATION Before piping on the whip, drizzle dimensional fabric paint over the caps of the lens case. (Make sure caps are removed before applying dimensional paint.) Screw caps back onto the case before applying whip and center embellishment.

Sweet Somethings Mini-Chalkboard

DESIGNED BY ALICE FISHER

Hang a cute chalkboard on your bedroom door or use it in the kitchen to leave notes for mom or your little brother. Sometimes a handwritten reminder is nicer than a text message especially if it's asking for a later curfew!

SKILL LEVEL

Beginner

MATERIALS

Mini chalkboard

Painter's tape

White acrylic paint

Paint brush

Craft wood circle

Hot-glue gun

Whip of your choice

Star-piping tip and piping bag

4 large mini erasers

8 small mini erasers

Pink dimensional fabric paint

TO MAKE SWEET SOMETHINGS MINI-CHALKBOARD

1. Protect chalkboard surface with painter's tape and paint the frame white. Let dry about 20 minutes.

2. Paint the craft wood circle white and let dry. Hot glue wood circle to the corner of the chalkboard's frame.

3. Using the star-piping tip, apply a thick swirl of whip onto the circle, slightly spilling off onto the frame of the chalkboard.

4. Embed larger mini erasers into the whip, then fill in with the smaller erasers.

5. Squeeze dimensional fabric paint over the frame in a loose drizzle. Let dry for 48 hours.

TIP This project can look really cute in a restaurant or kitchen. Find or make cabochons in the shape of your signature dishes to really get your guests salivating!

Girly Glam Compact Mirror

DESIGNED BY CASSIE PERRY

Pull this gem out of your purse next time you need to put on lipstick in public. You'll be the envy of all your friends!

SKILL LEVEL

Beginner

MATERIALS

Compact mirror

Glue

10–15 various cabochons

Rhinestones and flat-back plastic pearls

Tweezers or wax pencil

TO MAKE GIRLY GLAM COMPACT MIRROR

1. Plan out your design before gluing anything to the compact mirror case. *Trace the compact onto paper and lay out pieces in your desired design. Or, arrange embellishments on the case and snap a cell-phone pic to use as a guide when you're ready to glue.*

2. Working in small sections, apply glue to the outside of the compact and adhere embellishments. Fit larger cabochons close together to give it a dense look.

3. Fill in gaps with dots of glue and adhere small rhinestones or pearls into those spaces. Use tweezers or a wax pencil to place them accurately.

4. For maximum strength, let glue dry for 48 hours.

TIP If you don't have tweezers or a wax pencil, lightly touch the end of a toothpick in glue then tap the rhinestone for easy grabbing.

So Chic Sunglasses

DESIGNED BY ALICE FISHER

Buy a pair of inexpensive sunglasses and give them a miraculous make-over with small rhinestones, cabochons, and pearls. You will look like a million bucks when you turn cheap to chic!

SKILL LEVEL

Intermediate

MATERIALS

Sunglasses

Glue

Toothpick

12–16 small to medium cabochons (2 sets of each)

Small flat-back plastic pearls

Rhinestones

Tweezers or a wax pencil

TO MAKE SO CHIC SUNGLASSES

1. In order to achieve this orderly design, work on these sunglasses in a symmetrical fashion. Start in one corner and add an embellishment, then repeat the same element on the opposite side.
Use a toothpick to spread glue on the thin surface of sunglass frames. Using a toothpick will help keep the lenses and hinges free of adhesive.

2. Work your way across the top line of the sunglasses using cabochons in various sizes. Glue a medium-sized cabochon right in the center of the glasses, over the bridge of the nose.

3. Apply glue to the bottom half of one side of the frame and adhere small rhinestones and pearls. Use tweezers or a wax pencil to help with placement. Repeat for the other side.

4. For maximum strength, let glue dry for 48 hours.

TIP Keep your design very focused by using just 2 colors to embellish your glasses.

Fast and Fashionable Accessories

DESIGNED BY CASSIE PERRY

DecoDen cabochons are so pretty that sometimes you just need one alone to make a statement. Leave the whip and drizzle off of these dainty accessories that are so quick and easy to make.

SKILL LEVEL

Beginner

MATERIALS

Cabochons

Bobby pins

Metal ring blanks

Eye hooks

String, chain, or cord

Craft glue, such as Amazing Goop®

TO MAKE FAST AND FASHIONABLE ACCESSORIES

1. Apply the glue to each surface first and allow it to sit for 2 to 10 minutes before sticking the pieces together. Glue cabochons to bobby pins, ring blanks, and eye hooks.

2. Once cabochon is glued to its respective notion, let it dry for at least 24 hours.

TIP You can speed up drying time by applying heat with a hair dryer on low. Keep dryer at last 6 inches away from accessory.

Sweet Bangle Bracelet

DESIGNED BY ALICE FISHER

Arm candy has a whole new meaning with this almost edible bangle bracelet.

SKILL LEVEL
Beginner

MATERIALS
1" wide plastic bangle
Whip of your choice
Star-piping tip and piping bag
Candy cabochons
Rhinestones

TO MAKE CUTE CANDY BANGLE BRACELET

1. Pipe whip onto bangle in a wave pattern, moving the piping tip up and down along the height of the bangle. Work all the way around until bangle is covered.

2. Holding the bangle from the inside so as not to smudge the whip, begin placing the candy cabochons around the bangle, evenly spaced.

3. Once candy is in place, fill in around the pieces with rhinestones. Let dry for 48 hours before wearing.

TIP Go a step further by really covering every bit of visible surface with whip before attaching your cabochons— just be sure you can comfortably wear your new jewelry!

contributors

The following projects were supplied by contributors for inclusion in DecoDen Bling:

"Beach-Comber Phone Case" (p. 10) by **Rachael Beck**. More information on Rachael and her crafts can be found online at her Etsy shop, ShesoftheSea.

"Cool Azul Mosaic Phone Case" (p. 11) by **Kathy Cano-Murillo**. More information on Kathy and her crafts can be found on her website, craftychica.com.

"Upcycled Bling Tablet Case" (p. 12 A) by **Linnette Garcia**. More information about Linnette and her crafts can be found on her website, jewelrysugar.com.

"Plastic Fantastic Phone Case" (p. 13 A), "Chocolate Delight Phone Case" (p. 14 A), "Girly Glam Compact Mirror" (p. 26), and "Fast and Fashionable Accessories" (p. 28) by **Cassie Perry**. More information about Cassie and her crafts can be found online at her Etsy shop, KreativeKoala.

"Simply Sweet Phone Case" (p. 15) by **Ashley Vala**. More information about Ashley and her crafts can be found on her website, bitykitydecoden.com.

"Kitty Video-Game Case" (p. 16), "Glitzy-Girl Jewelry Box" (p. 19), "Cherry-on-Top Clutch" (p. 20), "Time, Sweet Time Clock" (p. 21), "Rainbow Garden Photo Frame" (p. 22), by **Cathie Filian** and **Steve Piacenza**. For information about Cathie and Steve and their crafts can be found on their website, handmadehappyhour.com.

"Pretty-in-Pink Trinket Box" (p. 17) by **Erynn Tanimoto**. More information about Erynn and her crafts can be found online at kawaiixcouturedecoden.com.

"Upcycled Bling Tablet Case, Rhinestone Variation" (p. 12 B), "Plastic Fantastic Phone Case, Rhinestone Variation" (p. 13 B), "Chocolate Delight Phone Case, Bunny Variation" (p. 14 B) by **Taylor Vasiliou**. More information about Taylor and her crafts can be found on Ebay by searching for her shop: Taylorshomemadecases2012.

resources

MICHAELS® STORES

Michaels.com

Silicone molds

Easycast Resin

Mod Podge DecoDen line

Fine glitters

Mod Podge

Embellishments like rhinestones, beads, charms, etc.

Dimensional fabric paint

Polymer clay

SOPHIE AND TOFFEE

http://sophieandtoffee.com

All Decoden supplies

ETSYSM

www.etsy.com

All Decoden supplies and cabochons

AMAZONSM

www.amazon.com

All Decoden supplies and cabochons

EBAYSM

www.ebay.com

Cabochons

Molds

Modeling clay

Tools

Findings

DecoDen whip

DELISH BEADS

www.delishbeads.com

Beads

Cabochons

Findings

ROCKIN' RESIN

www.rockinresin.com

Cabochons

IT'S CUTE

www.decoden-acc.com

All DecoDen supplies

If you like these projects, you'll love these other fun craft booklets

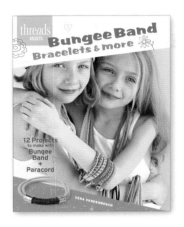

Bungee Band Bracelets & More
12 projects to make with bungee band & paracord

Vera Vandenbosch

Bungee cord is no longer just a tool—now available in a wide variety of colors and thicknesses, it's the perfect material for you to create beautiful bracelets and necklaces. The 12 projects in this booklet will show you exactly how to transform this stretchy material into runway-worthy designs for you to wear and show off.

32 pages, product #078048, $9.95 U.S.

Arm Knitting
chunky cowls, scarves, and other no-needle knits

Linda Zemba Burhance

Knitting your own scarf, cowl, or blanket is easier than you think, and with the brilliant new technique called arm knitting, it couldn't be quicker. Each of these 12 projects knit up in under an hour and only require a few skeins of yarn. Best of all, you don't need any tools—just bring your arms and hands! Go wild with the bright colors of the Fun Times Scarf, add a sophisticated layer to your date night outfit with the Evening Sparkle Tie-on Shrug, or just cuddle up with the Super Cozy Throw. Just know that your friends are going to want some of their own!

32 pages, product #078045, $9.95 U.S.

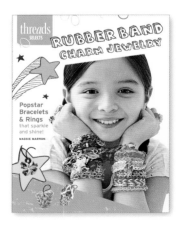

Rubber Band Charm Jewelry
popstar bracelets & rings that sparkle and shine

Maggie Marron

This booklet offers 15 great jewelry projects to make on or off of your loom—rings, bracelets, anklets, and even charms made out of nothing but rubber bands! Spice up your day the popstar way and let loose with these celebrity-inspired accessories. Learn how to make fishtails, starbursts, tulips, and so much more as you grab a little piece of the spotlight for yourself!

32 pages, product #078047, $9.95 U.S.

Shop for these and other great craft books and booklets online: www.tauntonstore.com

Simply search by product number or call 800-888-8286, use code MX800126

Call Monday-Friday 9AM - 9PM EST and Saturday 9AM - 5PM EST • International customers, call 203-702-2204